HI

MW00879919

The Count of Monte Cristo

Alexandre Dumas

Abridged and adapted by Janice Greene

Illustrated by Steve Moore

A PACEMAKER CLASSIC

GLOBE FEARON
EDUCATIONAL PUBLISHER
PARAMUS, NEW JERSEY

Paramount Publishing

Supervising Editor: Stephen Feinstein
Project Editor: Karen Bernhaut
Editorial Assistant: Stacie Dozier
Art Director: Nancy Sharkey
Assistant Art Director: Armando Baéz
Production Manager: Penny Gibson
Production Editor: Nicole Cypher
Desktop Specialist: Eric Dawson
Manufacturing Supervisor: Della Smith
Marketing Manager: Marge Curson
Cover Illustration: Steve Moore

Printed in the United States of America
3 4 5 6 7 8 9 10 99 98

ISBN 0–835–90989–1

GLOBE FEARON
EDUCATIONAL PUBLISHER
PARAMUS, NEW JERSEY

Paramount Publishing

Contents

Cast of Characters

Edmond Dantes	The hero of the novel, who is betrayed by his enemies. He triumphs over them with a plan of revenge.
Monsieur Morrel	A shipowner and Dantes' employer
Danglars	A ship's purser who becomes a rich banker; one of Dantes' enemies
Caderousse	Another of Dantes' enemies; the owner of a country inn and a scoundrel
Mercedes	Dantes' fiancée, who later marries Fernand
Fernand	Dantes' rival and betrayer; a fisherman who becomes a rich member of Parliament
Villefort	The public prosecutor who puts Dantes in prison
The Marquise	Mother of Villefort's first wife Renee, and Valentine's grandmother
Abbe Faria	A fellow prisoner who educates Dantes and tells him of a fabulous treasure
Maximilian Morrel	Son of the ship owner. He is in love with Valentine.
Albert	Fernand's and Mercedes' son
Franz	A friend of Albert. He is engaged to Valentine.
Luigi Vampa	An Italian bandit who is a friend of Dantes
Haydee	A young Greek woman who loves Dantes. Her father, Ali Pasha, was betrayed by Fernand.
Heloise de Villefort	Villefort's second wife. She poisons several people to get an inheritance for her son, Edouard.
Valentine de Villefort	Villefort's daughter and Heloise's stepdaughter. She is in love with Maximilian Morrel.
Benedetto	The illegitimate son of Villefort who poses as the rich Italian Andrea Cavalcanti
Noirtier	Villefort's father and Valentine's grandfather; a supporter of Napoleon

1 Betrayal

Marseilles, France, 1815

A crowd had gathered at the edge of the water. A ship, the *Pharaon*, was slowly coming into port. People in the crowd wondered what could be wrong. For the ship had an air of sadness about it.

One worried man left the crowd. He jumped onto a small boat and went out to meet the *Pharaon*. The man was Monsieur Morrel, the owner of the ship.

A sailor came to meet Monsieur Morrel as he climbed on board. The sailor was 19 years old, tall and slim, with jet black hair. He held his hat in his hand. He was the first mate, Edmond Dantes.

"Ah, it's you, Dantes," said Monsieur Morrel. "What's happened?"

"A terrible thing, sir," said the young man. "Captain Leclere is dead. He died of fever."

"And the cargo?" asked Monsieur Morrel with a concerned look.

"All is safe," said Dantes. "But here is your purser, Monsieur Danglars. He can tell you all you want to know. And now if you will excuse me, sir, I must bring the ship in."

Danglars walked up to Monsieur Morrel with a smile. The purser was about 25 or 26. He bowed to those who were above him and looked down on those below him. The crew disliked him as much as they liked Dantes.

"Well, Monsieur Morrel, I suppose you've heard our sad news," said Danglars. "The captain was a true man of the sea. He was well fit to carry the cargo of such an important man as you."

Monsieur Morrel was watching the crew. They worked smoothly and quickly under Dantes' orders. "Captain Leclere was a fine captain," he said. "But I'm happy to see young Edmond Dantes taking over so well."

Danglars looked at Dantes with hate. "I'm sorry to say so, sir," said Danglars, "but young Dantes made us lose more than a day on our trip. He made a stop on the Isle of Elba—for no reason at all."

"Dantes," said Monsieur Morrel, "come here, please."

The first mate walked over while Danglars stepped away. Monsieur Morrel said to him, "I wanted to ask why you stopped at the Isle of Elba."

"It was the wish of Captain Leclere, sir," said Dantes. "As he was dying, he asked me to take a package there to a Marshal Bertrand."

Monsieur Morrel looked around quickly. He took Dantes off to one side.

"How is Napoleon?" he asked. His voice was low and excited.

"He seems to be fine, as far as I could tell," said Dantes. "He came into the marshal's room while I was there."

"Good, good," said Monsieur Morrel. "You did well, Dantes."

"Thank you, sir," said Dantes. "And now I must ask you for two weeks' leave."

"To marry your fiancée, Mercedes?" asked Monsieur Morrel.

"First of all, and then to go to Paris."

"Take as long as you like," said Monsieur Morrel. "We won't put to sea again for another three months. But be sure to come back then. The *Pharaon* can't sail without its new captain."

"Captain!" said Dantes. His eyes flashed with joy. "Thank you, sir!"

Soon Dantes was free to leave the ship. He thanked Monsieur Morrel once more and hurried away. Danglars and Morrel watched him go. There was a huge difference in the way the two men looked at Edmond Dantes.

As quickly as he could, Dantes made his way to the little room where his father lived.

"Father!" he called.

The old man cried out. He fell into his son's arms. His face was pale.

"Father, are you sick?" cried Dantes. "Let me get you a glass of wine." He looked around the room. Its shelves were empty.

"There's no food," said Dantes. "How can that be? I left you 200 francs."

"That's true, Edmond," said the old man. "But remember we owed our neighbor, Caderousse. He wanted his 140 francs. He said if he didn't get it, he'd go to Monsieur Morrel."

"You lived for three months on 60 francs?" said Dantes. "May God forgive me!"

Just then they heard someone coming up the stairs. In a minute, Caderousse, the tailor, was at the door. He was a man about 25 years old, with black hair and beard. "So you're back, Dantes!" he said. His sharp white teeth glowed in a wide grin. "I've heard the good news! You're a very lucky young man."

"Yes," said Dantes. He tried not to let his voice grow cold.

Caderousse went on, "Of course, all your old friends are happy to see you doing well. And I know someone else who will be happy with your news."

That "someone" was Dantes' fiancée, Mercedes Herrera. Soon, after giving his father money for food, Dantes hurried to the village where she lived. Meanwhile, Caderousse went to join his friend Danglars in the tavern.

Mercedes was a beautiful young woman, with dark skin and soft eyes. Just now, she was standing against a wall. Across from her sat a young fisherman. He looked at her with both love and anger.

"Listen, Mercedes," said the young man. "Give me an answer!"

She said, "I've already answered you a hundred times, Fernand. I love you like a brother. But my heart belongs to Edmond Dantes."

"And will you always love him?" said Fernand.

"As long as I live," she answered.

Fernand said between his teeth, "And if he dies?"

"If he dies, so will I," she said.

"And if he forgets you?" asked Fernand.

At that moment a voice full of joy called from outside the house, "Mercedes!"

"There he is!" cried Mercedes. She ran outside and fell into Dantes' arms. The fierce sun of Marseilles covered them with its light. For a while they forgot everything else around them. Then Dantes felt Fernand's look of hate.

"Excuse me," Dantes said. "I didn't know there were three of us."

Mercedes said, "Don't you remember Fernand? He is your friend, because he is my friend."

"Ah, yes!" Dantes held out his hand to Fernand.

A look from Mercedes made Fernand take that hand. Then he turned and rushed from the house like a madman. "Oh, what can I do?" he thought.

"Where are you going in such a hurry?" called a voice. Fernand stopped. He saw Danglars and Caderousse sitting outside at the tavern. He sat down with them. The three men drank. Caderousse spoke of Dantes with envy. Fernand thought of him with hate.

After a while, Danglars thought, "It looks as though Dantes' luck will hold out. He'll marry a beautiful young woman. He'll become captain of the *Pharaon*. He'll have a laugh on all of us— unless. . ." He smiled. "Unless I take a hand in things."

Soon Dantes and Mercedes came walking by, and Caderousse called them over. Dantes told them he would be going to Paris soon. Danglars remembered what Dantes had brought back from the Isle of Elba. It was a letter. "He must be going to take that letter to Paris," thought Danglars. "That gives me an idea—a very good idea!"

The next day, all the sailors of the *Pharaon* arrived at the tavern. Even Monsieur Morrel came. They came for the betrothal feast of Dantes and Mercedes. Dantes felt so lucky and happy he could not believe it. But soon after everyone sat down to eat, the police and soldiers came. Dantes was arrested. He had no idea why.

Now let us go to another part of Marseilles, to a grand house. Another betrothal feast was taking place. Gerard de Villefort, the prosecutor for the king, was going to marry Renee, daughter of the Marquis and Marquise of Saint-Meran. He did not love her terribly, but he loved her enough. After all, her family stood high in the court of the king. And she was very rich. Villefort was a happy man.

The guests lifted their glasses to King Louis XVIII. "Those people who follow Napoleon are not like us," said the Marquise to Villefort. "They are not loyal to the king."

"But they have something else," said Villefort. "Napoleon is more than a man to them. He makes them equal with kings."

"You sound like a follower of Napoleon!" said the Marquise. "But we must excuse you. After all, your own father is for Napoleon."

Villefort turned red. "It's true my father supports Napoleon, Madame. But I am separate from my father. Even my name is different. His name is Noirtier. My name is Villefort—and I am for the king!"

"Bravo!" said the Marquise.

Just then, a servant said there was a message for Villefort—a note. Villefort took it and read that a man named Edmond Dantes had been caught with a letter from Napoleon.

Villefort said good-bye and hurried to the house where Dantes was being held. He asked Dantes a great many questions. Soon, Villefort made up his mind that Dantes was innocent. It was clear the young man had nothing to do with Napoleon. He had no idea what was in the package he had delivered or in the letter he was supposed to take to Paris.

At last Villefort said to Dantes, "I believe you have an enemy—the person who wrote me the note. But it seems you are telling the truth. You may go back to your friends."

"Do you mean I'm free to go?" Dantes' voice was filled with joy.

"Yes, but first give me the letter," said Villefort.

"It's in my papers, sir," said Dantes.

Villefort began to look through the papers. "To whom were you supposed to take the letter?" he asked.

"I was to deliver it to a Monsieur Noirtier sir, " said Dantes.

A thunderbolt could not have hit Villefort more suddenly. He thought, "If anyone learns about this letter to my father—it's the end of me!"

Villefort forced himself to speak calmly. He said, "I'm afraid this letter makes things more difficult. I can't let you go right away. I have to keep you here until tonight. But I am destroying this letter. This is the one piece of evidence against you."

"Oh, thank you, sir!" said Dantes.

Dantes was kept in the house until dark. Then several policemen came and opened his door. But he was not set free. He was taken in a boat to that great black rock far out from Marseilles. On that rock sits the terrible prison, the Chateau d'If. No man escapes from there.

2 A Terrible Promise

Soon after putting Dantes in prison, Villefort went to see King Louis XVIII. He told the king that Napoleon had plans to come to France. That is what was in the letter that Dantes was supposed to bring to Paris. But, of course, Villefort did not tell the king that the letter had been addressed to his father, Monsieur Noirtier.

Napoleon did come to France, and when he came, King Louis fled the country. Napoleon set up his Court of a Hundred Days. Because his father was a friend of Napoleon, Villefort was able to keep his job as prosecutor.

While Dantes was gone, Fernand was with Mercedes every day. He was very good to her, and she grew to like him more and more.

Then the German and the English armies rose up against Napoleon. Napoleon called for every man who could fight. So Fernand left, along with the others.

Mercedes was left alone. Day after day, she walked by the sea in tears. Her dear friend Fernand was far away. And Dantes seemed gone forever.

Finally came the great Battle of Waterloo, where Napoleon lost for the last time. Louis became king once more.

When Napoleon was taken prisoner by the king, Dantes' father lost all hope of seeing his son again. Five months later the old man died, and Monsieur Morrel paid for his funeral. That was a brave act since Dantes was in prison for supporting Napoleon. It was dangerous to help even the father of such a man.

Dantes knew nothing about what happened. All he knew were the four walls of his prison cell. For many months, he hoped he would be set free. After all, he had done nothing wrong. He begged to talk to someone. He begged to send a letter. He begged for books. Finally, he begged for a new cell, even a darker one, just for a change.

The years passed. For a long time, Dantes felt terribly sad and angry. He screamed with rage and threw himself against the walls of the cell.

He no longer felt like eating. He grew weak, and the day came when he could no longer stand. When he closed his eyes, he saw bright flashes.

Then one night, as he lay in the dark, he heard a scratching sound. The next day, he heard the sound again. That day, Dantes ate. His mind was filled with hope. The jailers would not work night and day. The sound must be another prisoner!

Using the handle from his food pan, Dantes began to dig at the mortar between the stones of the wall. After many days, he came to a large piece of wood which blocked his path. "Oh, my God!" he cried out. "Don't let me die with nothing to hope for!"

A voice said, "Who speaks of God and no hope at the same time?"

Dantes felt his hair stand on end. "Please!" he cried. "Speak to me again! Who are you?"

"Who are you?" said the voice.

"I'm a prisoner," said Dantes. "But I've done no wrong. Won't you tell me who you are?"

"I'm—I'm prisoner number 27," said the voice.

"Don't you trust me?" said Dantes.

"I might, for you sound too young to be a traitor," said the voice. "Hide your work well. Wait for me to come to you."

The next day Dantes waited. At last he heard the sound of falling dirt and stones. A man came through the hole and stepped into his cell.

Dantes threw his arms around him. Then he stepped back to look at the other prisoner. He was a short man, with a beard that came down to his chest. He looked about 65. The old prisoner was terribly sad. He had been digging

14

for years, hoping to find his way to freedom. Instead, he had only found another cell. But in spite of his sadness, he soon warmed up to Dantes.

The man was the Abbe Faria. He showed Dantes his cell and the wonders hidden there. He had made a knife from a candlestick and pens from fish bones. He had made paper from his shirts. On this he had written a book about Italy. The abbe had a dream of seeing Italy as one great empire. That dream had landed him in prison.

Dantes told the abbe his story. The abbe listened closely. Then he asked questions. He saw that Danglars and Fernand had been jealous of Dantes. It was they, along with Caderousse, who had gotten Dantes in trouble. And when Dantes told him that the prosecutor's name was Villefort, the abbe said, "You poor man!" He knew of Noirtier, follower of Napoleon. And he knew that Villefort was his son.

At last Dantes knew why he had spent years in prison. He told the abbe he must be alone for a while. He went back to his cell and lay on his bed for hours. When he got up, he had made a terrible promise—a promise of revenge.

When the two prisoners met again, the abbe said, "I am sorry I let you see into your past. I should not have told you all this."

"Why not?" asked Dantes.

The abbe said, "Because I see in your heart something that was not there before."

"Let us talk of something else," said Dantes. "You must teach me a little of what you know."

"Ah, my boy," said the abbe. "I don't really know so much. I know something of mathematics, physics, and history. I know three or four languages. That is all. It won't take more than two years for you to know all that."

Dantes wanted to begin right away. That night, they made a plan for his education. In a year, Dantes was a different man.

But the abbe had more on his mind than Dantes' education. He had made a new plan of escape. Outside their cells was a gallery with a window to the outside. A guard kept watch there, walking back and forth. They would make a new tunnel under the gallery floor. They would loosen the stones of the floor so the guard would fall through. Then they would tie him up and climb through the window.

For 15 months they worked on the new tunnel. Then, at last, they could hear the guard walking above them. The day of escape was close. But one afternoon as they worked, the abbe suddenly fell with a cry.

"What's the matter?" cried Dantes.

"A terrible sickness—a cataleptic fit," said the abbe. "I can feel it coming on. If I seem to be dead, bring my medicine. Give me ten drops."

Suddenly the abbe began to shake. His face turned purple. Then he lay still. He was white and cold as stone.

Dantes ran to get the medicine. It was a red liquid. He put ten drops in the abbe's mouth. Soon the color came back to the abbe's face. "This is the end," he said sadly. "I cannot move my right leg or arm. The next attack will kill me. You must escape alone."

"No!" cried Dantes. "We can still escape. I'll swim with you on my back."

"You could not swim more than 50 yards like that," said the abbe.

Dantes said, "Then I'll stay here. I won't leave you while you're alive!"

The abbe looked at the young man before him. "So be it," he said. "I thank you. And now you must go. I hear the jailer."

The next morning, Dantes came to see his friend. The abbe had a piece of paper in his left hand. He said, "On this paper is the secret to a great treasure hidden on the Isle of Monte Cristo. This was given to me by the man I worked for. Now I give it to you."

"That treasure belongs to you, my friend," said Dantes.

"You're my son!" cried the abbe. "You're the child of my years in prison."

Dantes threw his arms around the old man's neck and cried. A few days later, the old man was dead. A great sadness came over Dantes. Once more, he was alone! He thought, "The only way I'll leave prison now is when I die, like the abbe."

Then suddenly he had an idea. If he, rather than the abbe, was buried in a grave, he might be able to find his way to freedom. He hurried to the abbe's cell. The jailers had put the old man in a sack. Dantes brought the abbe's body to his own bed. Then he climbed into the sack. He had just finished sewing it closed when the jailers came.

They picked up the sack and carried it outside. Dantes waited to feel the dirt of a grave. Instead he heard the roar of the sea.

The jailers swung him back and forth. They counted, "One, two, three!" Dantes fell through the air. The fall seemed to never end. Then he hit the cold sea like an arrow. He screamed and the water closed over him.

3 Diamonds and Gold

Wildly, Dantes swung the abbe's knife. He cut open the sack and kicked himself up through the water. At last he reached the surface and gulped in the cold sea air.

He began to swim toward Tiboulen. After a time, he became very tired. He tried to float, but the sea became rough. A storm was blowing up. Suddenly Dantes felt something sharp. It was a rock. Land! He climbed on shore and slept.

When he awoke, it was still night. The storm roared about him. Lightning flashed, and he saw a fishing boat about to crash on the rocks. He called out, but it was too late. In the dark, he heard the cries of the men. He hurried down to the spot where he had seen the boat. He called out again, but only the sound of the sea answered him.

At last morning came. The sea was quiet now. Dantes looked out over the water and saw an Italian ship sailing toward Tiboulen. He got ready to swim to it. Then he saw one of the fishermen's caps in the water. He grabbed it and put it on. Now he had a story.

He swam out to the ship. Two sailors pulled him in and gave him food and drink. After a while, he asked, "What year is it?"

A sailor said, "What? Don't you know?"

Dantes replied with a laugh, "I was so scared when our boat crashed last night that I almost lost my mind. I still can't think clearly."

"Well," said the sailor, "it's 1829." Dantes had been in prison 14 years. A sad smile passed over his lips. He wondered what had become of Mercedes. Then he thought of his promise of revenge against Danglars, Fernand, and Villefort.

The ship's captain, who had been watching Dantes, said, "Now what shall we do with you?"

Dantes answered, "Do what you like. I'm a good sailor. I can take a ship into any harbor in the Mediterranean Sea."

A sailor asked the captain, "Why can't he stay with us, then?"

Dantes stayed. The ship turned out to be a smuggling ship. It sailed all about the Mediterranean, picking up goods from here and there. And it did not pay the taxes on these goods. Dantes passed the Isle of Monte Cristo many times, but he had no chance to go there. That was all right. He had learned to wait.

Then, after three months, Dantes got his chance. The ship's captain had made a plan to meet with another smuggling ship to trade stolen goods. As luck would have it, he chose the Isle of Monte Cristo as the meeting place. Nothing lived there but wild goats.

The two crews made their trade. After the other ship had left, Dantes went hunting and killed a wild goat. While the crew cooked it, Dantes looked around the island. Then he started back. The men saw him come running. Then, as they watched, he slipped on a rock and fell. They hurried over to him. Dantes had fallen about 15 feet. His knee and back were hurt.

"Just leave me a little food," he said, "and a gun and an ax, in case you can't come back right away. A day or two of rest will put me back on my feet."

As soon as the ship was out of sight, Dantes began to look for the treasure. He no longer had the abbe's paper, but the secret was in his head. Soon he was inside the cave he had read about. There, under a rock, he found a square stone. An iron ring was set into it. He used a branch as a lever to pull up the stone. Under the stone was a tunnel, with stairs that led to a second cave. It was here that Dantes found the chest of wood— the treasure chest.

His heart began to pound. He pushed the ax blade under the lid of the chest. The lid flew open. Dantes closed his eyes like a child.

When he opened them, he could not believe what he saw.

In the chest were bright gold coins. There were ingots of gold. There were diamonds, pearls, and rubies. Dantes let the glittering jewels fall through his hands.

He ran out of the cave like a madman. He ran about the island screaming, which scared the goats. Then he ran back inside to his treasure and fell on his knees and prayed. It was a prayer only God could understand.

After all these years, Caderousse was no longer a tailor in Marseilles. Now he was the owner of a country inn. One day he was standing in front of his inn, looking down the road. He was wondering if he would get any business at all that day, when he saw a priest riding up.

"You're Monsieur Caderousse, aren't you?" asked the priest. He had an Italian accent.

"Yes, sir," said Caderousse. Dantes had changed very much from the young sailor he once was. Caderousse did not recognize him in this disguise.

"Didn't you once live in Marseilles?" asked the priest.

"Yes," said Caderousse. "I've had this inn for several years now. But business is poor. And my wife is always sick. But how do you know so

23

much about me?"

"I'm here because of Edmond Dantes," said the priest. "I'm here to carry out his will."

"Dantes? Is he dead, then?" Caderousse asked.

"He died in prison, without hope."

"Poor boy!" Caderousse brushed away a tear.

Dantes watched him closely. "You must have been quite fond of him," he said, still disguising his voice.

"I was," said Caderousse. "For a while I was jealous. He was so happy. But now . . ."

"As Dantes was dying," said the priest, "he told me a prisoner—a rich man from England—had given him a diamond. Dantes said to me, 'I want to share it with those who once loved me. Sell it, and divide the money into five parts.' "

Caderousse's eyes were bright. "A diamond!" he said.

The priest went on, "Dantes told me, 'One of my friends was Caderousse. Another was Danglars. A third was my rival, but he loved me, too. His name was Fernand. Then there was my fiancée Mercedes. The fifth person was Dantes' father, who is now dead. I heard about it when I was in Marseilles."

Caderousse said, "Yes, poor man. He did nothing but wait for his son, who never came. He wouldn't see anyone. Finally, he let Mercedes and the ship owner, Monsieur Morrel, see him.

They sent for a doctor, but it was too late. The old man died of hunger and sadness."

Dantes turned away, trying to hide his tears.

Caderousse went on, "Monsieur Morrel paid off the old man's debts. He tried many times to get Dantes out of prison."

The priest said, "I hope God has made him rich and happy."

Caderousse smiled a bitter smile. "Monsieur Morrel is almost out on the street now. He has lost five ships in two years. His debts are enormous. But these other men Dantes thought were his friends?"

"You better watch what you say!" said a voice. It was Caderousse's wife. She was sitting at the top of the stairs.

"Maybe she's right," said Caderousse.

"Are you saying Dantes' friends were not true to him? Then perhaps they should not have a share of this!" The priest took the diamond from his pocket. It glittered before Caderousse's eyes.

Caderousse wiped his forehead. "You're right," he said. "It would not be just. But you must promise not to repeat what I tell you. These so-called friends are rich and powerful."

"Don't worry. Remember, I'm a priest. Now, tell me."

Caderousse told the priest what Danglars and Fernand had done, how they had told the prosecutor that Dantes was working for Napoleon. Wiping his forehead again, Caderousse said, "When I found out what they'd done, I wanted to tell the truth. But Danglars said I'd get in trouble, too.

"Danglars made a fortune during the war with Spain. Then he married a rich widow. Now he's Baron Danglars, with a great house in Paris.

"Fernand is rich, too, and a count. He joined the Greek war against the Turks, fighting on the side of the Greek leader, Ali Pasha. When Ali Pasha died, he left Fernand all his money."

"And Mercedes?" asked the priest.

"When Fernand left, she was all alone," said Caderousse. "Dantes was gone. His father would not see anyone, even her. When Fernand came back, she was happy. She thought this was love. They were married. Now Mercedes is rich and well-educated. She's one of the great ladies of Paris, but I don't think she's really happy. . . . They have a son, Albert." Caderousse sighed. "As you see, they have done well. Only I am poor. . . ."

"You're wrong, my friend," said the priest. "God remembers, sooner or later. Here's the proof." He gave Caderousse the diamond.

"For me alone?" asked Caderousse.

"For you," said the priest. "I know now that Dantes had only one true friend."

Next, Dantes went back to Marseilles. Dressed in the clothes of an Englishman, he went to the mayor. He said he was from the English banking firm, Thomson and French. He asked about Monsieur Morrel's debts.

A few weeks later, Monsieur Morrel sat at his desk, his head in his hands. His last ship, the *Pharaon*, had been lost in a storm.

Morrel's son, Maximilian, stood close by. "Is there really no money left, father?" he asked.

"Nothing," said Morrel, sadly. "I cannot pay my debts."

Maximilian set his teeth. "Our name will be dishonored," he said.

Just then, Morrel's daughter, Julie, ran into the room. "You're saved!" she cried. In her hand was a bill for 285,000 francs, marked "paid."

Morrel could not believe his eyes. "Where did you get it?" he asked.

"A man I've never seen before," she said. "He gave it to me and then he was gone!"

On a boat leaving Marseilles was Dantes. He said, "Let your heart be happy, Monsieur Morrel! And now good-bye to kindness. Like God, I have been kind to the good. Now let God give up his place to me—and I will punish the wicked!"

4 The Plan Begins

The two young men from Paris sat in their hotel room. One was Franz d'Epinay. The other was Albert, the son of Mercedes and Fernand.

The young men were not happy. Here they were in Italy for the carnival. They were rich and proud. In their well-made pockets were letters of recommendation. They were ready to meet the society of Rome. But they could not find a carriage to rent—not anywhere!

Just then the door of their room opened. The hotel-keeper put his head in. "Good news, gentlemen," he said. "The Count of Monte Cristo lives on the same floor as you. He has heard of your troubles in finding a carriage—and he has offered you two seats in his own."

Franz and Albert looked at each other. "What kind of a man is this Count of Monte Cristo?" asked Franz.

The hotel-keeper said, "It seems he's a very great lord. He comes from Sicily or Malta. I don't know which. But he's a very noble man—and rich as a gold mine."

The next day, Franz and Albert paid a visit to the count. As they walked into his rooms, their eyes opened wide. The rooms were grand indeed. Beautiful rugs covered the floor. The walls were hung with magnificent paintings. Great curtains hung before each door.

As they stood waiting, a door opened. A curtain was pushed to one side, and the Count of Monte Cristo (who was none other than Edmond Dantes) walked in. "Good morning, gentlemen," he said. "I'm sorry I was not able to help you sooner. I only just learned of your problem. I am very happy to be of service."

The young men bowed.

Dantes went on, "Before the carnival begins, there will be an execution. I hope you will join me for that as well."

"Who are they going to execute?" asked Albert.

"There were supposed to be two men. One man is a murderer. The other is a young bandit, a member of Luigi Vampa's band. But I have word that he shall be pardoned. It is just as well. The bandit was to have his head cut off. As a way to die, that's far too easy."

"Too easy?" asked Franz. "I don't understand you very well."

"Listen," said Dantes. His face had a look of hate. "Suppose a man has tortured and killed your father, your mother, your sweetheart. He has left your heart empty and bleeding. When his neck is cut, he feels a few seconds of pain. Do you think this pays you back for all he's done to you? That's not how I would pay him back!"

"What would you do?" asked Franz.

"If I had been made to suffer long and slowly, so would he. An eye for an eye, a tooth for a tooth," said Dantes.

"But," said Franz, "that makes you both judge and executioner. If you acted on that idea, it would be hard to stay clear of the law. Besides, hate is blind; anger is foolhardy. And revenge can turn against you."

"Yes," said Dantes, "if you're poor and foolish. Not if you're rich and smart. But come, gentlemen. We must leave for the execution."

As Dantes predicted, the bandit was set free. The other man was led up to the executioners. He bit and screamed. Albert closed his eyes. Franz sank into a chair, almost fainting. Dantes watched everything. He looked like an angel of revenge.

When Franz came to, it was all over. Dantes and Albert were putting on costumes. It was time for the carnival.

Crowds of people filled the streets. The costumes were fantastic. Enormous cabbages walked along. Heads of buffaloes rode on the bodies of men. Dogs walked on two legs. Sometimes a mask was lifted to show a beautiful face—a face one might want to follow.

Franz and Albert went out in Dantes' carriage. They passed one carriage full of ladies again and again. Albert threw flowers into the carriage. The next time they passed, one of the women threw her flowers to Albert!

"Well!" said Franz. "This looks like the beginning of something."

The next day, they saw the carriage again. The woman who had thrown the flowers lifted her mask to show Albert her face. She was beautiful. On the following day, Albert was beside himself. The woman sent a note saying she would meet him!

It was the end of the carnival. Everyone bought *moccoletti*, the carnival candles. As it grew dark, the streets became a sea of lights.

Albert met his beautiful woman at last. Franz watched them go off arm in arm, and as he watched, a bell rang. The carnival was over. Suddenly, every single *moccoletti* was blown out, and the streets fell into darkness.

The next morning, Albert had not come back. Franz was wondering when he would see his friend again when a man brought him a note. It said, "Four thousand piasters must be in my hands by six o'clock. If I do not have them, Albert will die. Luigi Vampa."

Franz did not have enough money with him. He hurried to Dantes' rooms. Dantes listened to Franz's story. "Where's the man who brought you the note?" he asked.

"In the street," said Franz. Dantes called out the window to the man waiting below. In a minute, the man was at Dantes door.

"Ah, it's you," said Dantes. The man was the young bandit who had been pardoned.

The bandit did not answer. He fell to his knees and kissed Dantes' hand. He had been told that Dantes was responsible for getting the pardon.

"I see you know I saved your life," said Dantes. "Now, tell me. How did Albert fall into Luigi's hands?"

The bandit said, "The young Frenchman was making eyes at his girlfriend, Teresa."

"That woman was Luigi Vampa's girlfriend?" asked Franz.

"Yes," said the bandit. "And now the young Frenchman is a prisoner in the catacombs."

Dantes turned to Franz. "I'm glad you came to me," he said, "or your friend's adventure might have cost him his life." He rang a bell and told the servant to bring his carriage.

Soon they were at the catacombs. The bandit led them down a dark tunnel under the ground. They came to a large room, where about 20 men stood guard. The light of a lamp shined on their guns. Next to the lamp, one man sat and read. He was Luigi Vampa, the head of the band.

Dantes walked into the room. In seconds, every gun was turned at him.

"My dear Vampa," said Dantes. "Is this the way you say hello to a friend?"

"Put down your guns!" Vampa called to his men.

When Vampa learned that Albert was a friend of Dantes, he set the young man free. After they had left the catacombs, Albert said to Dantes, "I'll never forget that I owe my life to you. If there is anything I can do . . ."

Dantes laughed. "You don't owe me so very much," he said. "But I had made up my mind to ask of you one thing."

"What is it?" asked Albert.

"I have never been to Paris," said Dantes. "If you could introduce me . . ."

"Of course!" said Albert, his voice joyful.

Albert, Franz, and Dantes shook hands. To Franz, Dantes' hand felt as cold as a dead man's. When Franz and Albert were alone, Franz said, "The Count of Monte Cristo is a very strange man. I'm worried about your meeting him in Paris."

"What?" asked Albert. "Are you mad, Franz?"

Franz said, "Mad or not, I'm still worried."

5 Paris

At Albert's house in Paris, several men awaited the arrival of another guest. One of them turned to Albert and said, "Who is this Count of Monte Cristo? And where is Monte Cristo, anyway? I have never heard of such a place."

"I think I can answer that for you," said a handsome young captain in uniform. This was Maximilian Morrel, son of the ship owner. "Monte Cristo is a little island, a grain of sand in the Mediterranean Sea."

"I say there is no Count of Monte Cristo," said another man. "Look! It is half-past ten, and he's still not here."

But just as the clock finished striking the hour, a servant said, "His Excellency, the Count of Monte Cristo!"

Dantes walked in without a sound. His clothes were simple, but perfect.

The men sat down with the new guest. By the time he had told them of the emerald he had given the Pope, they were hanging on his every word. When the breakfast was over and the men were leaving, one of them said, "The count is the most amazing man I have ever met."

Albert then took his guest to the salon to meet his parents. Fernand was now 40, but looked 50. He looked at the man before him with a friendly gaze. It was clear he did not recognize the count as Edmond Dantes.

Dantes held out his hand. "What an honor it is to meet you," he said. "For not only have you been a great soldier, but now you do a second service to your country as a member of Parliament!" Fernand smiled.

"And here is my mother!" said Albert. "Mother, are you all right?"

Dantes turned to see Mercedes. She was holding onto the door, her face white.

"What's the matter?" Fernand asked his wife. "Is the salon too hot?"

"I'm all right," said Mercedes. She smiled. "It's only that my heart is shaken to see the man who saved my son's life. I bless you, Count, and I shall always be in debt to you."

Dantes bowed low. His face was even whiter than Mercedes'.

Mercedes then said, "Will you do us the honor of spending the rest of the day with us?"

"I would like to very much," said Dantes, "but this is my first day in Paris. I haven't even seen my new house yet."

Soon Dantes said good-bye to Albert and his parents. He took a carriage to his new

home. It was noon now, the time he liked to visit with Haydee.

Haydee was a beautiful young Greek woman, with soft black eyes and lips like coral. After he escaped from prison, Dantes rescued Haydee and her mother from slavery in Turkey. Dantes had been her protector ever since. Dantes said to her, "You grow more beautiful every day, Haydee. There are many young men of Paris who would be happy to meet you."

Haydee said in her soft voice, "But I don't want to be with anyone but you."

Dantes said, "I have taken care of you since you were a child. But you're a woman now. I cannot stand in the way if some handsome young man . . ."

"There is no man more handsome than you. And I've never loved anyone but you and my father."

"Do you remember your father, Haydee?" asked Dantes.

"He is always here," said Haydee, putting her hand on her heart. "But my love for you is different."

"Poor child!" said Dantes. "In ten years I'll be old and you'll still be young. You'll love me as you love your father."

Haydee smiled. "You are wrong, my lord," she said.

6 The Poison Seed

A few days later, Dantes rang for his servant. The man came into Dantes' study.

Dantes said, "You are very good at throwing the lasso, are you not?"

The servant nodded, his face proud.

"Could you stop two horses that were running away?" asked Dantes.

The man smiled.

"Very well," said Dantes. "A short time from now a carriage will pass. It will be driven by two gray horses, running away at top speed. You must stop them in front of my door."

The servant nodded. He went outside to wait.

Suddenly there was the sound of a carriage coming at great speed. A minute later, Dantes and his servant could see it. The horses were running wild. The coachman could not stop them.

As the carriage reached the front of the house, the servant threw his lasso. It caught the front legs of one of the horses. The servant was dragged a few feet until the horse fell. Running up quickly, the servant grabbed the other horse by the neck. It cried out in pain and stopped in its tracks.

Dantes ran up to the carriage. Inside were a woman and a boy of eight. Dantes carried them inside the house.

"You're safe now, Madame," he said.

"But my son!" cried the woman. "Look how pale he is! Please, sir, send for a doctor!"

"I don't believe he's hurt, Madame," said Dantes. "He has only fainted." He opened a small chest and took out a flask. Inside was a blood-red liquid. He put one drop on the boy's lips. A moment later, the boy opened his eyes.

"Oh, Edouard!" the mother's voice was filled with joy. She turned to Dantes. "Where am I? And to whom do I owe so much happiness, after so much fear?"

"I am the Count of Monte Cristo," he said.

"So you are the count I have heard so much about! And I am Heloise de Villefort."

Dantes smiled and bowed as if he did not know this was Villefort's second wife.

Suddenly he turned to Edouard, who was reaching for the red liquid. "Don't touch that, my boy!" said Dantes in a sharp voice. "That liquid can be poison."

Heloise pulled her son close, her face full of fear. But when the fear had gone, she gave the red liquid a long look.

Heloise was so interested in the medicine that Dantes promised to send her some. As she thanked him again and said good-bye, she added, "Please don't forget to send my medicine!"

Dantes thought, "I think the seed I planted will grow."

That same day, Monsieur de Villefort paid a visit to Dantes. Villefort did not visit many people; only those few he thought worthy of him. Villefort thanked Dantes, in his stiff way, for saving his wife and son.

Dantes said, "I know you do not visit people often, so I am honored. But that honor is not as important as what I wanted—which was for you to come to me." His voice was cold as ice.

Villefort stepped back in surprise.

Dantes went on, "Of course, to you, people's positions are important. But such people are only given positions by ministers or kings. God has placed some above ministers and kings. He has given them missions far more important."

Villefort drew himself up. "I suppose you are one of those extraordinary people?" he asked. He wondered if Dantes was insane.

"Yes, I'm one of them," said Dantes coldly. "Kings belong to one country. My country is the world itself. Only death can keep me from my mission, which is to reward, and to punish."

Villefort said, "I admire you, count. You are truly a powerful person. When you say only death can stop you, I believe you. I must leave you now, but I hope you will one day know me better. For I myself am not an ordinary man, not at all."

When Villefort had left, Dantes said to himself, "My heart is full of poison. I must take the antidote." And he went to visit Haydee.

While Dantes was visiting Haydee, a young woman paid a visit of her own. It was Valentine, daughter of Villefort and his first wife, Renee. Valentine was 19, tall and slender, her hair a rich brown.

Valentine walked quietly to the edge of her garden. "Maximilian!" she called softly.

"I'm here," said the voice of Maximilian Morrel. He was hiding on the other side of the garden wall. "But what's the matter?" he said. "You sound sad tonight."

Valentine replied, "They have told me that the marriage must take place in three months! Oh, Maximilian! I can't bear the thought of marrying Franz when it's you I'll always love."

Maximilian said, "So soon! I thought your stepmother didn't like Franz."

"You don't understand," said Valentine. "It's not that Heloise doesn't like Franz. She doesn't want me to marry at all. For when I do, all my mother's and grandmother's money will come to me. And when my grandfather, Monsieur Noirtier, dies, his money will as well. Heloise's son, Edouard, will get nothing. However, father says the marriage must take place. But listen, someone's calling me! It's time to give grandfather his dinner!"

Maximilian kissed her quickly on her fingers, and off she ran.

7 Money and a Good Name

A carriage stopped before Dantes' door. In it was a richly dressed man. His hair was long and black, but it did not hide the many wrinkles on his face. This was a man of 50 or 55, trying to look 40. It was Baron Danglars, the banker.

Danglars was shown into the salon. In a moment, Dantes came in. Danglars met the man known as the Count of Monte Cristo with a smile. He never guessed it was the same man he had sailed with on the *Pharaon* many years ago.

"I have your letter, count," said Danglars, "but I don't quite understand your wish. It says you want unlimited credit with my firm."

Dantes said, "What don't you understand?"

Danglars answered, "This word 'unlimited'. . ."

"The reason I wrote 'unlimited' is that I don't know how much I'll need," said Dantes.

Danglars said proudly, "Oh, don't be afraid to ask. You may be sure that I have plenty. Even if you were to ask for a million . . ."

"If I only wanted a million francs, I wouldn't have bothered to open an account," said Dantes. "A million! Why I carry at least that much with me." And from his card-case he drew out two bonds for five hundred thousand each.

A man like Danglars cannot be given a light tap. He must be hit over the head—hard. This blow had its effect. Danglars stared at Dantes in a daze. Then he opened an account for Dantes for an "unlimited" amount of money.

That night Dantes had a guest we have not seen before. He was a young man with a red beard, blond hair, and black eyes. This man was the illegitimate son of Villefort. Dantes discovered from a servant that long ago Villefort had abandoned this son. Some kind people had rescued the boy. But as he grew into a young man, he became a criminal. This was all very good news to Dantes.

The young man had a strange letter in his hand. What the letter said was this: "You are poor; you have a hard life ahead of you. Would you like to be free and rich? Would you like to have a good name? If so, go to see the Count of Monte Cristo. You will be given papers to prove you are a noble, rich Italian. Then you will be able to present yourself to Paris society." Also in the envelope was the count's address and a check for five thousand francs.

When the young man arrived, Dantes began to coach him. His new name would be Andrea Cavalcanti, and he would claim to be the son of a major. He was to stay at a grand hotel in Paris.

Trunks full of fine clothes waited for him there. Soon he would meet the great families of Paris.

The young man learned very quickly. Dantes was quite happy with him. It was late at night when the young man's education was finished. Dantes said good night to him and went upstairs with a smile. "There goes a fine scoundrel!" he said to himself.

Dantes' servants had brought a carriage for the young man. Just as he was climbing in, he felt a hand on his shoulder. He turned to see a man's face, with eyes that glittered and teeth like a wolf's.

"What do you want?" said the young man.

"A ride in your fine carriage would be very nice," said Caderousse, for indeed it was he. The two got in. Caderousse said: "I'm happy to catch up with you, old friend. It looks like you've come into good times, Benedetto."

Benedetto frowned at hearing his real name. He pulled at his red beard.

Caderousse went on, "You remember how we used to share when we were in prison. What a big eater you were! You were a bit greedy, I'm sorry to say."

Benedetto said, "Who are you to talk about greed? You're the one who got 5000 francs for that diamond the priest gave you. Then you killed the diamond trader, so you could have

47

both the money and the diamond!"

Caderousse replied, "Perhaps your new friend in that grand house back there would like to hear why you were in prison."

"Don't make me angry, Caderousse!" said Benedetto.

Caderousse's hand moved quietly to his pocket. His finger touched the trigger of a small pistol. Benedetto's hand went behind his back. Gently, he opened his long Spanish knife. The two looked at each other.

Finally Caderousse said, "Listen, Benedetto. I'm not going to bother your new friend. But it will cost you."

"All right," said Benedetto. "How much do you need?"

"With 150 francs a month," said Caderousse, "I'd be very happy."

"Here's 200," said Benedetto. "I'll be getting money every month. You can come see me then."

"Good," said Caderousse. "Good-bye, Benedetto!" He jumped out of the carriage.

Benedetto sighed. He said to himself, "I suppose it's impossible to be perfectly happy in this world."

It was a few days later when Dantes stopped by to visit the Villefort family. As he was leaving, he said, "I am going now to see something I have

always wanted to see."

"What is it?" asked Heloise.

"A telegraph," said Dantes. "It is a wonder to me—those messages flying through the air for miles and miles. And one man sitting at one end, while another man sits at the other end . . ."

"Which line are you going to visit?" asked Villefort.

Dantes said, "The line from Spain, I suppose. I have heard that one is the busiest."

The next day, Danglars learned that King Don Carlos was trying to return as Spain's ruler. As quickly as he could, Danglars sold his Spanish bonds. He lost a lot of money, but he was happy to get rid of them.

Then, one day later, Danglars read this in the newspaper: "Yesterday's news of Don Carlos's return to Spain is false. The news was the result of a mistake in a telegraph message, caused by fog."

Spanish bonds rose to double their price. Danglars had lost one million francs.

When one needs money, it never hurts to have one's daughter marry a rich man. And soon it was learned that Danglars' daughter, Eugenie, would marry a young Italian named Andrea Cavalcanti. Danglars knew Andrea was a very rich young man. After all, the Count of Monte Cristo had told him so.

8 "Murder in Your House!"

Villefort was alone in his study when he heard someone crying. Opening the door, he saw the Marquise, Valentine's grandmother. The old woman walked in and sank into a chair. "Oh, what a terrible thing!" she said. "I'll die, too! Yes, I will die, too!"

"What has happened?" asked Villefort.

"My husband is dead," said the Marquise.

"Dead? So suddenly?" asked Villefort."

"Yes," said the Marquise. "He died in a minute—just like that. I can no longer cry. It seems I have no more tears left."

The Marquise was put to bed. Soon she fell asleep. An orange drink, her favorite, was put on a small table beside her. She did not wake until the next day.

When Villefort came to see her, she said, "You have plans to marry Valentine to Franz, don't you?"

"Yes, Madame," said Villefort.

"Franz is the son of the General d'Epinay, isn't he?" said the Marquise. "Wasn't he killed by men who were for Napoleon?"

"Yes," said Villefort.

"Noirtier is Valentine's grandfather, and he was a strong supporter of Napoleon. Doesn't that bother Franz?"

"Not really," said Villefort. "After all, Franz was a child when his father was killed."

"Then the marriage must take place right away," said the Marquise, "because I don't have long to live."

"You cannot mean that!" said Villefort.

"It is true," said the Marquise. "I know this sounds impossible, but I'm sure of what I say. A ghost came to me last night. I even heard it move my glass."

"You must not think of such things," said Villefort. "You'll live a long time, yet."

"Never!" said the Marquise. "And now I want to see a notary. I want to make sure all my money goes to Valentine."

"Oh, Madame," said Villefort. "It is not a notary you need, but a doctor."

"A doctor?" said the Marquise. "I'm not in pain, only thirsty." She reached for her drink and drank it down. Then she turned over on her pillow. "The notary!" she said, "The notary!"

A day later, the Marquise was dead. The doctor walked outside with Villefort.

Villefort said, "Don't try to make me feel better, doctor. My pain is too deep. She's dead! Dead!"

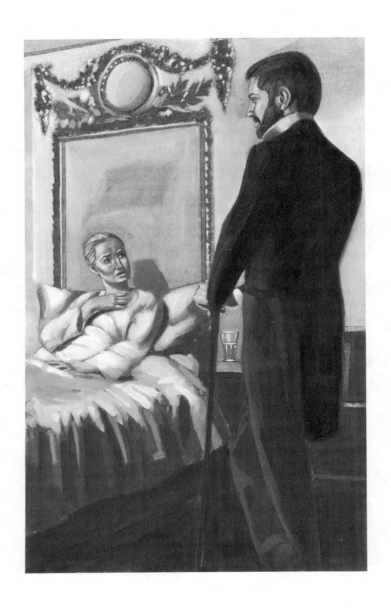

"That's not why I brought you out here," said the doctor. "I have something I must tell you–something terrible. The Marquise died of poison."

Villefort said, "Oh, it's impossible! I must be dreaming! Tell me, doctor. It must be a mistake!"

"I don't think so," said the doctor. "Is there anyone who might gain from the Marquise's death?"

"No, of course not!" said Villefort. "All her money will go to Valentine—oh, no! I'd rather die myself than think such a thing!"

"Listen," said the doctor. "Our job now is to protect those who are alive. Let us bury this terrible secret in our hearts. But we must watch. This business may not stop here. If we find the one who is guilty, I trust you will act as you see fit. After all, you're a prosecutor."

"Thank you, doctor!" said Villefort. "Thank you from the bottom of my heart!" And as if he was afraid the doctor might change his mind, he led him quickly back into the house.

Two days later, the Marquise was buried next to her husband. And a week after that, Franz was asked to come to the Villefort house to sign the marriage papers.

The papers were to be signed at two o'clock. Valentine felt desperate. Her father took her arm and led her down to the salon.

The notary was already there. So was Franz. Just as they were about to begin, the door opened. It was Barrois, Noirtier's old servant. He said, "Monsieur Noirtier has something he must tell all of you."

He brought in Noirtier in his wheelchair. Some years ago, Monsieur Nortier had suffered a stroke. Now he could not move or make a sound. He spoke with his eyes. Only Valentine, Villefort, and the servant could understand him.

Noirtier raised his eyes. This was a sign that he wanted something. Valentine said, "What do you want, grandfather?" A small flame of hope began to burn in her heart. Noirtier knew she loved Maximilian, and he did not like Franz.

Valentine began to go through the alphabet. At the letter "s," Noirtier signaled "yes," by closing his eyes.

Valentine asked, "Sa? Se?"

"Yes," signaled Noirtier.

Valentine put the dictionary in front of Noirtier. Beginning with "se," she moved her finger down the page. At each word, she looked at Noirtier's eyes. At the word, "secret," he signaled "yes."

"Is there a secret you wish to show us?" asked Valentine. The flame of hope burned higher.

Noirtier signaled "yes."

Villefort coughed nervously. He said, "Father,

I'm sure this can wait until after the marriage papers are signed."

Noirtier's eyes flashed. "No! No!" he blinked.

Valentine used the alphabet and the dictionary once more. What Noirtier wanted was something in a "secret drawer." He looked at his old servant.

"Does he know about the secret?" asked Valentine.

"Yes."

The old servant went and brought back some papers tied with a black ribbon.

"To whom shall I give the papers?" he asked.

Noirtier looked at Franz.

Franz took the papers. "The date on these papers is February 5, 1815!" he said. "That is the day my father was killed."

Franz began to read. His father, a supporter of the king, had found himself in the middle of a secret meeting with several men who were for Napoleon. Franz's father insulted one of the men. There was a sword fight. As Franz read, his voice began to shake. It was awful to watch a son read about the death of his father.

Franz came to the end. He put down the papers, his face white. "You!" he cried. "Monsieur Noirtier! You were the one who killed my father!"

Noirtier looked back at Franz with a majestic expression.

Franz sank into a chair. "I cannot marry the granddaughter of the man that killed my father," he groaned.

Villefort turned and ran, for he had felt like choking out what little life lay in his father's stubborn heart.

Some days later, Noirtier, Valentine, and Maximilian were having a secret meeting in Noirtier's room. The old servant was there, too, having some lemonade. It was a hot day, and he had gone on a long errand.

Maximilian was dizzy with happiness. He had learned that Franz had broken off the marriage.

In a shy voice, Valentine told Maximilian what her grandfather had planned. Noirtier would move to his own apartment, with the old servant and Valentine. When she was of age, she and Maximilian could marry.

Suddenly, the old servant, who was walking to the door, staggered and reach out for something to hold onto. "He's going to fall!" cried Maximilian. He caught hold of the old man.

"Help me!" cried the servant. "I feel like I'm on fire! Don't touch me! Don't touch me!"

Just then Villefort walked in. He looked at the old servant in a daze, his mouth open.

Maximilian hid behind a curtain.

"I'll send for the doctor!" cried Valentine. She left the room, taking Maximilian with her. Villefort, watching the old servant with horror, did not see Maximilian leave.

The servant fell to the floor. His arms and legs were so stiff it seemed they would break.

The doctor came, but there was little he could do. When the attack ended, he asked the old servant what he had eaten and drunk. He learned that he had drunk some of Noirtier's lemonade. Then, to Valentine's great surprise, he asked her to leave.

Soon another attack came, and this time it was the end.

"There is death in my house!" cried Villefort.

"There is murder in your house!" said the doctor. "The old servant was poisoned. This time I'm sure of it! And the poison was meant for Noirtier."

"But he drank that lemonade, too," said Villefort.

"He did," said the doctor. "Nobody knows this, but I have been treating Noirtier with small amounts of this poison for several months. His body has become used to it. Now, Villefort, you must know who the guilty one is!"

"Oh, have mercy on Valentine, doctor!" said Villefort.

"Ah, you name her yourself!" said the doctor.

"Listen to me," said Villefort. "It cannot be her!"

"The old servant told me it was Valentine who brought the lemonade," said the doctor. "And she is the one who will inherit Noirtier's money—just as she has inherited the Marquise's money!"

"What if you have made a mistake?" cried Noirtier.

The doctor was silent. Then he said, "Very well, I'll wait. But if someone else in your house becomes sick, don't call me. I will never come here again. Good-bye, Monsieur de Villefort."

9 "One Gone!"

"I need more money, old friend," said Caderousse to Benedetto. "If I had 500 a month I could have a maid."

Benedetto said, "All right, you can have your 500 francs. But it's going to be hard for me."

"I don't see why," said Caderousse. "There seems to be no end to the money you get."

Benedetto seemed to have been waiting for Caderousse to say this. He turned his head so Caderousse could not see the gleam in his eye. He said, "Yes, the Count of Monte Cristo treats me very well."

"He's very rich, isn't he?" said Caderousse.

"Very. You should see his house," said Benedetto.

"Tell me about it," said Caderousse.

Benedetto did. He even drew Caderousse a plan of the house. He drew every wall, door, and window. "The windows are so big a man could fit through them," said Benedetto.

"Where do the servants sleep?" asked Caderousse.

"In a separate building," said Benedetto.

Then Benedetto told Caderousse that the

count was going away the following night.

The next day, Dantes received a note: "The Count of Monte Cristo is warned that an enemy will break into his house tonight."

When night came, Dantes and his servant waited in the dark. At a quarter to 12, he heard a scratching sound. Someone was cutting the window glass with a diamond. The sound made Dantes shiver.

Just then the servant touched his arm and pointed. Outside, another man watched and waited.

Dantes walked silently toward the room where he heard the thief. He wanted very much to know who this enemy was.

The man was inside now trying to open Dantes' desk. His face was lit by a small light. "Caderousse!" said Dantes to himself.

Dantes walked silently away. When he came back, he was dressed as a priest. Underneath his clothes was a coat of steel.

He whispered to his servant, "Stay here unless I call you." Then he stepped into the room.

"The priest!" said Caderousse.

"You remember me," said Dantes. "And now, I see, you're trying to rob the Count of Monte Cristo's house."

Caderousse said, "I had to do something! I am so poor!"

"Poor!" said Dantes. "You didn't kill the diamond trader because you were poor! And you're not here now because you're poor. You're living off Benedetto. Tell me the truth! Tell me everything, and I'll take pity on you."

Caderousse looked at him with fear. "You seem to know everything already," he said. "But it's true. Benedetto is called Andrea Cavalcanti now. The Count of Monte Cristo gives him all the money he wants. And he'll have even more money when he marries Eugenie Danglars."

"And you would let him do that?" said Dantes.

"Why should I stop a friend from doing well?" said Caderousse.

"You're right," said Dantes. "You're not the one who should warn Danglars. I am."

"You won't tell him anything, priest!" cried Caderousse. He drew his knife and struck at Dantes' chest. But to his surprise, the knife bounced back. Dantes took Caderousse's arm and twisted it. Caderousse fell with a cry of pain.

"Take this pen and write what I tell you," said Dantes.

Caderousse sat and wrote: "Monsieur Danglars—Andrea Cavalcanti, whom you plan to make your son-in-law, is a fraud. He is a convict who escaped from the prison of Toulon with me. He calls himself Benedetto, for he does not know his real name."

Dantes took the letter. "Now, go," he said coldly. "If you get home safely, then I'll believe God has forgiven you. And I will forgive you, too."

Caderousse said, "You frighten me to death!"

"Go!" said Dantes. He pointed to the window. Caderousse climbed out the window. Just as his feet touched the ground, he saw an arm holding a knife. Before he could do anything, the knife struck him in the back.

"Help!" called Caderousse.

Dantes and his servant came running with a lantern. They carried Caderousse inside. Dantes turned to his servant and said, "Go get a doctor. Then get Monsieur Villefort, the prosecutor."

Caderousse said, "It's too late for a doctor. But bring me the letter to Danglars. It was Benedetto. He stabbed me, and I want Danglars to know."

Dantes brought him the letter. It was hard for Caderousse to hold a pencil. A drop of Dantes' red liquid helped him go on.

"There," Caderousse said at last, "now he'll be punished. And you'll be punished too. You didn't do your duty as a priest. You should have stopped Benedetto from killing me."

"I!" said Dantes with a smile that made Caderousse's blood run cold. "After you tried to kill me? If you had felt sorry for what you'd done, I might have saved your life. But I let God's will be done."

"I don't believe in God, and neither do you!" said Caderousse.

"There is a God," said Dantes. "The proof is that you're about to die. But I stand before you, rich and happy and well."

"Who are you?" said Caderousse, weakly.

Dantes bent down to his ear. He whispered, "I am . . ."

Caderousse cried out, "Oh God in heaven. I see now you are the true judge of men on earth. Forgive me, lord!"

Then he closed his eyes. Caderousse was dead.

"One gone!" said Dantes.

Ten minutes later the doctor and Villefort were at the house. There they found the priest, praying for the soul of Caderousse.

10   "Don't Kill My Son!"

Fernand did not read the paper that morning. Perhaps it was just as well, for an article in it said: "This paper has just learned of a strange event that took place in the Greek and Turkish war. It seems a French officer betrayed the Greek leader, Ali Pasha, and let the Isle of Yanina be taken by the Turks. The officer was Fernand Mondego, who is now a count and member of Parliament."

When Fernand arrived at Parliament the next day, one of the members rose to attack him in a speech. At the first words about Yanina, Fernand turned pale. His attacker called for an investigation. Gathering his courage, Fernand said he would answer the charges that very night.

When Fernand returned, he told the Parliament how he had tried to save Ali Pasha from the Turks. He showed them a ring Ali Pasha had given him as a sign of trust. But sadly, Fernand said, he had not been able to save Ali Pasha, or his wife and daughter.

The members of Parliament nodded. Fernand had answered the charges well.

Then the chairman said, "Gentlemen, I have just received a note. It seems there is a witness who has information to give us."

The chairman brought in a woman. She took off her veil and looked around her. She said, "I am Haydee, daughter of Ali Pasha."

Fernand felt as if a thunderbolt had opened an enormous hole at his feet. The chairman asked Fernand, "Do you recognize this woman?"

"No," he said. "This is a plot by my enemies."

Haydee cried, "I recognize YOU! You betrayed my father! It was because of you that he died! Murderer! You have the blood of my father on your forehead! Look at him! All of you!"

The words were spoken with such a pure sound of truth, that all eyes went to Fernand. Fernand put his hand to his forehead, as if blood were really there.

The chairman said to Fernand, "Do you wish the investigation to go on? Shall I send members of Parliament to Yanina?"

Fernand tore open his coat as if it were choking him. "No," he said in a flat voice. He ran from the room like a madman. The members of Parliament listened to his footsteps die away. Then every one of them voted "guilty."

When Albert heard what had happened to his father, he was extremely upset. He learned from a friend that Monsieur Danglars had recently sent a letter to Yanina asking questions. Albert went to face Danglars.

Danglars told him that the Count of Monte Cristo had advised him to write the letter. Albert decided that the count was behind the whole thing. He made up his mind to kill the man who had ruined his family's name. That very night, he found Dantes at the opera and challenged him to a duel. The two agreed to meet at eight o'clock the next morning in the woods.

At home, Dantes got ready. His servant brought him his pistols. He looked them over with care, though he knew he would win. Few men were a better shot than he.

Just then, his servant brought a woman in. It was Mercedes.

She said, "I beg you, Edmond Dantes, don't kill my son!"

"Madame, I promised vengeance against Fernand. If Albert wants to fight for his father's name, so be it," said Dantes.

"But I'm the one who's guilty," said Mercedes. "If you want vengeance, then punish me. For it was I who could not wait for you. It was I who could not stand to be alone when you were in prison."

"And why was I in prison?" said Dantes.

"I don't know," said Mercedes sadly.

Dantes unlocked a drawer and took out an old

paper. "Because of this letter, which Danglars wrote and Fernand sent," said Dantes.

Mercedes read. "Oh, no!" she cried.

"I bought this letter for 200 francs," said Dantes. "That was cheap, for it proves the reason for my vengeance."

Mercedes fell to her knees. "You must forgive! Forgive, for my sake!"

Dantes lifted her up and said, "You're asking me to go against God! He brought me back from a living death so I could punish them!"

"Take your vengeance," said Mercedes. "But take it on those who are guilty! Not on my son!"

Dantes held his head in his hands.

Mercedes said, "Must I see the man I loved become the murderer of my son?"

A sob burst from Dantes's throat. The lion had been tamed.

"Very well," said Dantes. "He shall live."

Mercedes kissed his hand. "Thank you," she said. "Thank you, Edmond. You're still the man I've always loved."

When she left, Dantes thought to himself, "You won't have much longer to love me, Mercedes." For if he could not kill Albert, then he must die himself. Albert had challenged him. If Dantes lived, it would be in shame.

The next morning, Dantes was first to arrive at the woods. With him was Maximilian. Franz was there, waiting for Albert. At eight o'clock, Albert rode up. He was pale and his eyes were red. It was easy to see he had not slept at all.

He walked up to Dantes. "Count," he said, "I have learned of the terrible thing my father did to you years ago. I believe you were right to punish him. And I thank you for not doing more than you did!"

Dantes lifted his eyes to heaven in thanks. He knew Mercedes had told her son everything.

"And now," said Albert, "if you accept my apology, please give me your hand."

Dantes, his eyes full of tears, gave the young man his hand.

When Dantes returned home, Haydee ran to meet him, her face filled with joy. Dantes began to hope for something he had never believed in before: that there might be another love in his life. Perhaps he might be happy once again.

Just then, the door opened. A servant said Fernand had come. As Dantes walked into the salon, Fernand said, "I know now you are my enemy! And since my son will not fight a duel with you, it is I who must." His face was full of rage.

"Very well," said Dantes.

"But first," said Fernand. "Tell me who you are. You know everything about me. You have opened up the dark of my past. You call yourself the Count of Monte Cristo. Who are you, really? I want to say your name as I put my sword through your heart!"

Dantes's eyes glittered fiercely. He ran from the salon and threw off his coat and vest. He put on a sailor's cap and shirt, returned to the salon, and stood before Fernand.

Fernand cried out in terror, "Edmond Dantes!" Then he ran from the room.

Fernand's carriage took him home. As he went up the stairs to his room, he heard two people coming down. He hid behind a curtain. He heard his son's voice say, "Courage, mother, this is no longer our home."

He listened as their carriage drove away. He looked out the bedroom window, hoping for one last look at all he had loved in this world. But neither his wife nor his son looked back.

A few minutes later, a shot rang out and Fernand was dead.

11 Vengeance and Doubt

The Danglars's house was filled with guests. Tonight the marriage contract between Danglars's daughter, Eugenie, and Andrea Cavalcanti (who was, of course, Benedetto) would be signed. Only one guest was missing— Monsieur de Villefort.

"It's very annoying," said Madame Danglars to her husband. "It's because of the robbery and murder at the Count of Monte Cristo's house. They've found some new evidence."

"I'm afraid it's my fault, Madame," said Dantes, walking up to her. "I found a letter that seems to have been written by the man who was killed." Everyone around him began to listen.

"It seems the letter was addressed to Monsieur Danglars," Dantes went on.

"To me!" said Danglars.

Just then the salon was full of noise and confusion. Benedetto began to move quietly toward the door. A police officer walked up to Danglars. "Which gentleman here is Monsieur Cavalcanti?" he asked. "He's an escaped prisoner from Toulon. He's also accused of murdering Caderousse."

Everyone looked around. Benedetto was gone. He did not get far, however. He was soon caught and arrested a short way from Paris.

A few days after these events, Dantes took five million francs from his account with Danglars. The same day, the commissioner of hospitals came to withdraw five million also. Danglars said he would have the money tomorrow.

As the man left, Danglars said, "Idiot! I'll be far away when you come tomorrow!" Then he locked the door, burned some of his papers, and checked his passport. "Good," he said, "it's valid for two more months."

Maximilian was worried. Valentine was not herself.

"I'm not really sick," Valentine told him. "I just don't feel like eating. Grandfather's been giving me some of his medicine. He says it will help."

But as she was walking downstairs, a cloud seemed to pass before her eyes. She rolled down the last three steps. Maximilian picked her up and set her gently in a chair.

Valentine opened her eyes. "How silly! Can't I even stand up anymore?" Then her eyes closed and her head fell back on his arm.

Maximilian rang the bell cord to call the servants. He waited until they came and then left at a run. It was to the Count of Monte Cristo that he turned for help.

When he told Dantes what was happening, the older man answered him coldly. "I think the justice of God has come to the house of Villefort," he said. "Turn your eyes away, and let justice do its work."

"Turn away! But I love her!" cried Maximilian. "I love her!"

"What?" said Dantes. "You love the daughter of that man!" He let out a cry like that of a hurt lion.

Maximilian stepped back in fear. He had never seen such an expression on a man's face.

Soon Dantes was calm once more. He said, "I laughed like an avenging angel at what evil men do to one another. Now I have been bitten by the snake I was watching."

He turned to Maximilian. "Don't lose hope," he said. "I'm here to watch over you."

Maximilian said, "Your coolness frightens me! Do you have power over death itself? Are you more than a man?"

Dantes smiled gently. "I can do much, my friend. Go now; I need to be alone."

One night soon after this, while Valentine was in bed, a man opened her door. She thought it was another one of her dreams.

"It's the Count of Monte Cristo," she said.

"Yes," said Dantes. "I'm here to protect you, and save you for Maximilian."

"Maximilian!" she said. "Did he tell you about us?"

"Yes," said Dantes. "Now listen. The medicine from your grandfather has saved you so far. But the murderer is still at work. Are you ready to see who it is?"

Valentine nodded, her face full of fear. "I think I just heard a noise," she whispered.

"Pretend you are sleeping," he said. "Courage!"

Valentine lay in silence for a long time. Then someone came into the room. It was Heloise, her stepmother. She poured something into Valentine's water glass and walked quietly out of the room.

Soon, Dantes came back to Valentine. "Do you know, now?"

Valentine groaned. "I can't believe it!" she whispered.

"Can you speak out against your stepmother?" Dantes asked.

"I'd rather die than do that!" said Valentine.

"Then you must trust me," said Dantes. "Even if you wake up in a coffin, believe I will come to you soon. Believe I am watching over you every moment. Believe it as you believe in Maximilian's love."

He handed her a tiny pill. She looked at him,

then swallowed. "And now good-bye, Valentine," he said. "You are saved." He watched her fall asleep as the narcotic took hold.

A few hours later, the doctor said Valentine was dead. Villefort's heart was broken. Noirtier seemed to scream from his silent body. Maximilian, who learned the news a few hours later, was beside himself. Only Heloise was calm, until she saw the doctor testing the liquid in Valentine's glass. Then she fainted.

Noirtier let Villefort know he wanted to see him alone. Afterwards, Villefort told the doctor, "My father has told me who the murderer is. Justice shall be done in three days."

Dantes, again disguised as the priest, prepared Valentine's body to be buried.

For the next two days, Villefort worked without resting on the case of Caderousse's murder. Then, on the morning of the third day, he got ready for the trial. A servant brought him a cup of hot chocolate, sent by his wife. He drank it down without stopping. It was almost as if he hoped it was poisoned. For at the moment, it seemed easier to die than do what he was about to do.

He went into his wife's room and said, "Where is the poison you use?"

Heloise made a choked sound. "I—I don't understand," she said.

Villefort said, "I asked you where is the poison? The poison you used to kill my parents-in-law and Valentine?"

Heloise's voice shook. "Am I speaking to my husband—or to a judge?"

"To a judge, Madame. To a judge!"

The woman hid her face in her hands.

Villefort went on, "But you must have another poison—one more gentle, more deadly. With this poison you can escape the punishment you deserve!"

Heloise let out a scream of fear. "No!" she cried.

"Oh, don't be afraid," said Villefort. "I will not hurt your good name—or mine or my son's! But justice must be done!"

"What can you mean?" cried Heloise.

"I was put on this earth to punish the guilty," said Villefort. "I would send any other woman to hang. With you I will have mercy. Where is the rest of your poison?"

"Oh, forgive me! Let me live!" cried Heloise.

"You're a coward," said Villefort.

"I'm your wife!"

"You're a murderer!"

Heloise fell at her husband's feet.

"I am going to court now," said Villefort. "If I find you here when I return, you will be in prison tonight."

She looked at him, her face white. Only her eyes were alive. They glittered with a terrible fire.

Villefort walked out, locking the door behind him.

The courtroom was crowded. Many were curious about the young, handsome Andrea Cavalcanti, who was accused of murdering Caderousse.

Benedetto was brought in. The magistrate said, "What is your name?"

Benedetto stood up. "Excuse me, sir," he said. "I will answer all your questions, but I wish to answer that one later."

The magistrate was surprised. "Very well," he said, "What is your profession?"

Benedetto's voice was calm. He said, "I began as a forger. Then I was a thief, and not long ago I became a murderer."

A storm of anger burst from the courtroom.

"And now," said Benedetto, "I can't tell you my name, because I have had many. But I can tell you my father's name."

"Tell us the name of your father then," said the magistrate.

Benedetto said, "His name is Villefort."

It took the magistrates five minutes to bring the court to order. Then Benedetto told how his father had abandoned him, and how he was raised by kind strangers. But though he was with good people, he grew up evil and turned to crime. The courtroom listened in silence.

"Can you prove any of what you say?" asked the magistrate.

"The proof?" said Benedetto, laughing. "Look at the prosecutor, Monsieur de Villefort. Ask him for the proof!"

All eyes turned to Villefort. Under the weight of those looks, he staggered to the center of the courtroom. His hair was wild and his face showed the marks of his fingernails. "There is no need for proof," he said. "The vengeance of God has struck me."

Villefort left the courtroom in a daze and drove off in his carriage. Suddenly, he saw Heloise's fan on the seat of the carriage. The sight of it was like a flash of lightning on a dark night.

"Heloise! Now she might be getting ready to leave me! And I was going to punish her," Villefort said to himself. "How did I dare! Me! Oh, no, she'll live! We'll leave France. I'll tell her everything. . . . We'll be together forever—a marriage between a tiger and a snake."

"Faster!" he called to his driver. "Faster!"

"It was because of Edouard that she did it all," Villefort said to himself. "The heart of a mother who loves her son can't be all bad. She must live, and her crime will pale beside mine!"

The carriage stopped. Villefort was home. He jumped out and hurried up the steps. A few minutes later, he was staring at the dead body of Heloise on the bedroom floor. Then he discovered the body of Edouard. Next to the boy was a note from Heloise which said: "You know I was a good mother. It was for my son that I became a criminal. A good mother does not leave without her son."

Some minutes later, Villefort came into the room where Noirtier was sitting with Dantes. He was again disguised as the priest. Upon seeing Villefort's wild look, Dantes knew what had happened in court.

Villefort said, "Why have you come here today? To pray for Valentine again?"

Dantes said, "I've come to tell you that you've paid your debt to me. From now on I will pray to God not to punish you any further."

Villefort stepped back in horror. "That's not the voice of the priest!" he cried. "You're the Count of Monte Cristo!"

"Think further back," said Dantes. "I am the ghost of a man you put in the Chateau d'If."

"You're Edmond Dantes!" cried Villefort. "Then come with me!" He took Dantes' arm and led him to where Heloise and Edouard were lying.

"Look, Edmond Dantes!" cried Villefort. "Are you happy now?"

Dantes went pale at the terrible sight. He knew he had gone too far. Villefort looked at his wife and son. He let out a loud scream and then a long burst of laughter. Dantes looked at him in horror. Villefort had gone mad.

Then as though he were afraid the walls of the house would fall on his head, Dantes hurried out to the street. For the first time, he doubted he had the right to do what he had done.

12 Vengeance and Peace

Dantes left for Marseilles, taking Maximilian with him. The poor young man took no comfort in seeing his old home. Without Valentine, there was no sunshine anywhere.

While Maximilian visited his father's grave, Dantes found Mercedes. She had come to Marseilles to say good-bye to her son Albert, who was joining the military.

He found Mercedes in tears. "I had no one but my son," she told him. "And now he has left me."

"He did the right thing," said Dantes. "He will make a life for himself now—a good one."

"I thank you again for saving him," said Mercedes. "I know you had planned to kill him."

"I am only an agent of God, Mercedes," said Dantes. "When God set me free from prison, it was part of some great plan. From that day, I knew no peace. I made myself vengeful and cold, or rather blind and deaf like Fate itself."

"Enough, Edmond," said Mercedes. "Now tell me good-bye."

"Before I leave you, Mercedes," said Dantes, "tell me what you want."

Mercedes said. "Only for my son to be happy."

Dantes said, "Pray to God to keep him from death, and I will do the rest."

"Thank you, Edmond."

As Mercedes watched the ship carry Albert away, she softly whispered Edmond's name.

Dantes was sad and full of doubt after leaving Mercedes. Had his vengeance against his enemies been just?

His next visit was to the Chateau d'If. It was no longer a prison. A guide led Dantes into his old cell. His heart beat wildly. He thought, "No! I began to doubt because I was beginning to forget. But now I feel again that pain in my heart. The thirst for vengeance returns."

Next Dantes was shown the cell of the Abbe Faria. "The old man had written a book on pieces of cloth," said the guide.

"Go get it for me!" cried Dantes.

The guide brought the book. Dantes took it from his hands. The first thing his eyes fell on were the words "Thou shalt tear out the teeth of the dragon and trample the lions underfoot, thus saith the Lord."

Dantes thought, "I was right! The teeth of the wicked must be pulled! Those who are deadly must die! This is a sign to me that my vengeance was just!"

He pulled out a wallet with ten thousand francs inside and gave it to the guide. Then he hurried away, holding the book to his chest.

When he saw Maximilian again, he said, "I must go to Italy. Will you wait for me? And meet me at the Isle of Monte Cristo when I return?"

"I'll do what you wish," said the sad young man.

Meanwhile, Danglars had arrived in Rome. He stopped at the banking firm of Thomson and French. There, he got five million francs—money that belonged to his creditors. The next day he set out for Vienna. In the carriage, Danglars fell into a happy sleep. When he woke, he looked for a town, but saw none. He began to worry. "Where are we going?" he asked. The driver answered in Italian, which Danglars did not understand. He grew more and more frightened.

At last the carriage stopped. Danglars was led into a long cave. Inside a great stone room, men with guns stood guard while one man, the leader, sat and read.

By this time, Danglars knew he was in the hands of the bandit, Luigi Vampa, whom Albert had told him about long ago.

Danglars was put into a cell to sleep. When he woke the next morning, he looked at his wallet. He still had all his money. "What strange bandits," he thought.

He was hungry. When he asked for food, a man

carried in a chicken on a silver tray. Danglars began to cut up the chicken.

"Excuse me, Excellency," said the young bandit. "But one should pay before eating."

"And how much do I owe for this skinny chicken?" said Danglars.

"Only 100 thousand francs, Excellency," said the bandit.

"Very funny," said Danglars. He turned back to his chicken. But the bandit stopped him.

"We never joke, Excellency," said the bandit. He took the chicken away.

Danglars' stomach had never felt so empty. A half hour later, he asked again for food. The bandit would be happy to bring some bread— but it cost as much as the chicken. At last Danglars' eyes were open. He paid the hundred thousand francs and ate.

After that, Danglars told them he would not give them another penny. He held out for two days. Then he broke down and began to eat— and pay. After twelve days, he had only fifty thousand francs left. Then a strange thing happened to a man who had given away so much. He felt he must keep the rest of his money no matter what. He had wild hopes that somehow he and his money would be saved. And so he stopped eating.

After four days, he was hardly alive. Finally, he

asked for a bit of bread for a thousand francs. But the bandit did not answer.

On the fifth day, Danglars called for Vampa. He said, "Take my money and let me live here. I'm not asking to be free. I only ask to live."

"Do you repent, at last, for all the evil you have done?" said a voice.

Danglars felt his hair stand on end. He saw a man standing in the dark behind Vampa. "Yes!" he cried. "I repent!"

"Then I forgive you!" The man stepped into the light.

"The Count of Monte Cristo!" cried Danglars.

"No, I am the man you betrayed, the man who forgives you now because he himself needs to be forgiven. I am Edmond Dantes!"

Danglars cried out and fell to the floor.

"Stand up!" said Dantes. "You will live. Your two friends weren't so lucky. One is dead and the other has gone mad. Keep the money you have left. I have given the money you stole back to your creditors. Now, eat and drink."

Danglars was given a fine meal. Then he was left on the side of the road. There, he spent the night. When morning came, he heard the sound of a river. He walked toward it. As he bent to drink, he saw that his hair was white.

Meanwhile, Dantes sailed away from Italy to the Isle of Monte Cristo. When Maximilian arrived, Dantes was already there. He had set up a room in a beautiful grotto.

"Welcome to Monte Cristo!" said Dantes. The young man seemed sadder than ever. The very life seemed to have gone out of his eyes.

"Maximilian has suffered enough," thought Dantes. "He has earned his happiness."

In the grotto, Dantes served a fine dinner. Afterwards, he gave Maximilian a liquid to make him sleep. Then he brought Valentine in to see him. In his sleep, Maximilian dreamed of her, and his lips moved a little.

"He's calling you in his sleep," said Dantes. "Death tried to keep you apart, but happily I was there and I won over death! You two must never leave each other again on this earth."

Overcome with joy at seeing Maximilian again, Valentine kissed Dantes' hand.

"Oh, thank me!" said Dantes. "Tell me again how I've made you happy. You can't know how much that takes away my doubt!"

"I thank you with all my heart!" said Valentine. "Dear Haydee can tell you how happy this makes me. It was she who helped me wait."

"Do you love Haydee?" asked Dantes hopefully.

"With all my heart!" said Valentine.

"Then I have a favor to ask you," said Dantes. "Look after her like a sister, for now—for now

she'll be alone."

"Alone?" said a voice behind him. "Why?"

Dantes turned around. Haydee was standing behind him.

"Because you must take your place in the world, Haydee," said Dantes. "You are the daughter of a prince."

Haydee turned pale. In a choked voice she said, "You're leaving me?"

The sound of her voice made Dantes shake. "Can it be true?" he cried. "Would you be happy to stay with me?"

Haydee said, "I love you as I love my life!"

Dantes felt his heart swell. He opened his arms, and Haydee ran into them.

"Then stay, my angel," said Dantes. "I wanted to punish myself for my revenge, but I see God wishes to forgive me. With you I will begin to live again, and be happy." He put his arm around her waist, and they left the grotto.

Valentine bent over Maximilian. She said, "Wake up, my darling, and look at me."

Maximilian let out a cry. He rose up, then fell to his knees, thinking he saw an angel.

The next morning, there was a note from Dantes. It said: "Maximilian, a boat is waiting to take you to Noirtier. He is waiting for his granddaughter, Valentine. My house in Paris is the wedding present which I give to you.

"Tell Valentine to pray now and then for me. Like the devil, I thought for a moment I was equal to God. But now I know that the greatest power and wisdom are in His hands alone.

"As for you, Maximilian, this is why I have let you suffer as you did: only a man who has truly suffered can be truly happy.

"Live, then, and be happy. And know that all human wisdom is in these words: Wait and hope. Your friend, Edmond Dantes."

Just then the young couple saw a white sail some distance from the island. "Who knows if we'll ever see them again?" said Maximilian.

"My darling," said Valentine, "as he told us, we must only wait and hope."